Coals of Fire

Therefore if thine enemy hunger, feed him; if he thirst, give him drink: for in so doing thou shalt heap *coals of fire* on his head. Be not overcome of evil, but overcome evil with good. —Romans 12:20, 21.

COALS OF FIRE tells the stories of men and
women who practiced doing good for evil. They
didn't just talk about loving their enemies; they lived
what they talked about. These are the kinds of
stories that make you remember how you felt when the boy
you detested in school gave you a piece of chocolate
cake the day you forgot your lunch. They make
you remember how well you slept the night you invited
the neighbor girl along to visit the zoo, a whole week after
her dad had shot your pet cat in his chicken pen.
You will remember the shame you felt when coals of fire
burned on your head. How sorry you were down
inside when your enemy did you a good
turn. You will remember those coals you heaped on
the head of your enemy, or the ones you
knew you should have and never did.
These people believed that love does no ill to its neighbor.
These people lived their love. Because they lived
their love they nursed sick refugees and gave
them warm coats. Because they lived their love they
sat behind jail bars without Bibles. Because
they lived their love they had their heads
cut off and were drowned. They lived heaping
Coals of Fire. Some died heaping them!

Coals of Fire

By

Elizabeth Hershberger Bauman

Illustrated by Allan Eitzen

HERALD PRESS
SCOTTDALE, PENNSYLVANIA

Christian Peace Shelf Series

The Christian Peace Shelf is a series of books and pamphlets devoted to the promotion of Christian peace principles and their applications. The editor, appointed by the Mennonite Central Committee Peace Section, and an editorial board, from the Brethren in Christ Church, General Conference Mennonite Church, Mennonite Brethren Church, and Mennonite Church, represent the historic concern for peace within these brotherhoods.

COALS OF FIRE
Copyright © 1954 by Herald Press, Scottdale, Pa. 15683
Library of Congress Catalog Card Number: 53-12197
International Standard Book Number: 0-8361-1350-0
Fourth Printing, 1971
Printed in the United States

Contents

Overcome evil with good.

ROMANS 12:21

An Ill Wind*

"Methinks this west wind bodes us no good," said William Rotch in an undertone to his wife, as he turned from the open window one morning in the summer of 1778.

"Why, Father, what harm can come from the west wind?" inquired twelve year old Thomas, who was always hearing things he was not expected to hear. "I thought the west wind was our friend, and brought the whaling ships safe to port."

* From *The Friendly Story Caravan*, collected by a Committee of the Philadelphia Yearly Meeting of Friends, Anna Pettit Broomell, Chairman. Copyright 1935, 1948, 1949, by Anna Pettit Broomell. Published by J. B. Lippincott Company. Used by permission.

"Yea, son, so it was in the old days, but, alas, we peaceful Nantucket folk can no longer ply our trade. Thou knowest, not a whaling ship has gone out for many a day. My fear is that today's wind may give a British privateer a chance to enter our Sherburne harbor."

"What? Not a full-rigged ship with guns and armed men? Why should they come to Nantucket? They know well that we are no fighting folk."

"True, my boy. Yet we be known as a thrifty community, and might be worth a visit. These privateers plunder where they can."

"Joe Macy told me that vessels flying the British flag have been sighted off the coast a dozen times during the past month."

"That is so, but they could not enter our harbor on the east wind that fortunately for us has been blowing all this long while. I shall go down into the town to see what tidings there be. Nay, stay thou with thy mother and sisters while I am gone. This may be a serious matter."

Without further words, William Rotch put on his broad-brimmed Quaker hat and strode down the street.

Ahead of him groups of anxious and excited townspeople were rapidly moving toward the wharf. Many of the old sea captains had their spy glasses with them the better to observe the formidable ship coming before the wind into the harbor, all her white sails set, and a wicked array of guns, visible even to those watchers who had no spy glasses. At the masthead floated the Union Jack, and the decks seemed to be crowded with gunners and sailors.

Old Asa Prindle offered his glass to William Rotch without comment. William looked through it at the tall ship as she came about, spilled the wind from her flapping sails, and prepared to anchor where her guns could best command the defenseless town. He could easily see a fine-looking officer directing the maneuvers, and borne by the stiff wind across the water, the boatswain's voice could be heard giving orders to lower away a boat from the ship's side.

Into this boat presently descended the crew, and then the fine-looking officer already noticed by William Rotch. After him followed six men with side-arms. Rowed by powerful strokes of the oars, the boat rapidly approached the wharf.

"No doubt of it now. They come for plunder," said old Asa.

"Suppose I talk with the commander on behalf of the town?" suggested William. "If I can get him to come to my house it may be well, for with the privations our people have undergone on account of the war someone might speak from his heart and anger our visitors into even worse measures than they contemplate."

"Our fate is safer in thy hands, William, than in our own. Do as seems best to thee, good neighbor."

"So say we all," came in many voices from the crowd surrounding William and old Asa.

The ship's boat made for the lee side of the wharf. With a boat-hook she was held to the tall piles while the painter was made fast. Out jumped the officer and his bodyguard of six armed men. William Rotch advanced to meet him with the friendly greeting that a loved and long-expected visitor might receive.

"This is William Rotch who bids thee welcome to Nantucket, friend. What may thy name be?"

"Sir Conway-Etherege, in the King's service," replied the officer, stiffly.

"I invite thee to come to my house—and thy friends likewise," said William, regarding calmly the six men with two pistols apiece in their belts.

"My men will await my orders, here," replied the officer.

Sir Conway-Etherege evidently thought his way was smoothed before him by this encounter with a friendly Loyalist inhabitant. He moved off beside William along the pleasant street up to a row of substantial looking houses.

William led his guest to the middle one of three large dwellings and bade him enter. It was nearly noon.

"I would like thee to take dinner with me."

"Thank you, with pleasure."

William then presented his guest to his wife and introduced his children, before they sat down together to a homely, ample meal. The younger Rotch children's eyes were shining with suppressed excitement, but they heeded their mother's hasty instructions to ask no questions, given when, to her astonishment, she saw her husband bringing in this unknown and possibly dangerous guest to share their dinner.

William treated the commander kindly and seemed to enjoy his conversation. The islanders had, as the officer knew, been cut off from contact with the outside world by the war. The officer furnished the news of the day, the current jests, and even the idle gossip of the mainland as it had come to him through English channels. From time to time he regarded William quizzically, as if he did not quite know how to approach his errand, although it was foremost in both their minds.

Finally they rose from the table. With the manners of his station in society, Sir Conway-Etherege made Elizabeth Rotch a flowery speech of appreciation, bowed over her hand and kissed it respectfully, at which Thomas had some ado to keep from snickering. The children followed their mother from the room.

"I take it, Mr. Rotch, from your signal courtesies to me, that you are on the King's side. Can you tell me how and where I had best begin the day's work? As you must know, I command yonder privateer, which has gone up and down the coast bent on plunder. Very successfully, too. We take pains to see that our guns rake all the important structures and districts of a town before we enter upon negotiations. As you see, your little hamlet is completely at our mercy. I anticipate no unpleasant resistance."

"There will be none," said William.

"Then how and where do you advise me to begin? The afternoon is advancing."

William smiled.

"I don't know of a better place to begin than here in my house. I am better able to bear the loss than anyone else. We have a store of silver plate, good, serviceable blankets, also linens; and in the cellar, supplies of food of various kinds. Thou art mistaken in supposing me to be on the side of those engaged in warfare."

Sir Conway-Etherege was greatly taken aback. He gazed at William with unconcealed curiosity. Never had he run across a man of his sort.

"Are there any more men like you on Nantucket?"

"There are many better men," answered William.

"Do you say so, indeed! I'd have to see them before I could believe it."

"Then come with me. I shall be glad to introduce some of our islanders to thee."

The officer followed William down the steps and out into the street again. This was a new experience to the commander of the privateer, and he did not know what to make of it.

Presently they entered a store where merchandise was sold. The store did not have a prosperous air, for the towns-people had little money for trade these days. Yet it had once done a large business, and was spacious and well-stocked.

William led the officer to the proprietor and introduced them.

"Our visitor wants to know what sort of people we are. I tell him that last winter thou wert the distributor of four hundred barrels of flour among the poor on the island. And yet I doubt if I, or any man, knows the full extent of what thou hast done to help the needy."

Amazed at this generosity on the part of a man with his living to make, the officer entered into conversation with the proprietor who told him of gifts of money which had found their way from William Rotch's pockets to households in distress, without anyone's suspecting him of being the donor. William hurried the officer out of the door at this. Further down toward the wharf they entered a store that sold dry goods.

"Good day, Peter," said William. "This officer from yonder ship in the harbor wishes to meet the man who gave away blankets, dress goods, and stout shoes last winter when the poor were in dire want."

"He might better turn around and meet thee, William. None of us has done what thou hast done. We but follow thy lead."

The face of William was rosier than even the brisk west wind had made it, as he led the officer out again into the street.

"My friends are modest," he said. "I can better afford to help others than they can. Dost thou care to cross the street and meet more of our people?"

"Thank you, no. I find it hard to believe that there are

three such men as you in the world. A whole street full of them would be almost too many. Thank you for your courtesy and forbearance. Farewell, my friend. I shall not forget Nantucket."

With that the officer grasped William's hand and shook it heartily. He looked once again up the leafy, beautiful street, and out toward the white-capped harbor where his ship with its deadly guns lay threateningly at anchor.

Groups of men were still watching and talking on the wharf. The sailors and the armed bodyguard were puzzled to know what had delayed their commander so long. Here he was coming at last. Well, the excitement of looting and plundering was worth waiting for. As Sir Conway-Etherege came briskly toward them, they saluted. His orders were quick and short. The sailors took their places at the oars, and rowed the officer back to his ship. The ship weighed anchor, trimmed her sails, and to the surprised relief of all Nantucket, sailed peaceably out of sight.

Perfect love casteth out fear.

I John 4:18

At the Wrong End of the Rifle

Edward Richards stopped dead in his tracks. Up and down the streets the newsboys were calling out the evening paper's glaring headlines:

"United States Enters the Great War!

"Country's Call to Arms!"

For two and a half years countries in Europe had been fighting, and Edward had guessed that the day would come when his own nation would join in the struggle. April, 1917, it came, and it made his heart beat quickly.

The young Quaker went his way, thinking seriously. What would he do? He believed that no good could ever come of killing his enemies. He hated the very thought of using a gun or a bayonet. He thought, too, about the times he and his friends had talked it over together. They did not

agree with him. If their country called, they would be patri-
otic and fight.

"The only way to be sure we are safe is to get rid of the
enemy," they argued.

"I think you are right," replied Edward. "We need to get
rid of our enemies. But killing them isn't the way to get rid of
them. That's not *real* victory. When you are so kind and
friendly that your enemies begin to love you instead of hating
you—that's real victory. Being friendly is the best way to get
rid of any enemy."

"Sounds very nice," his friends said, "but just wait until
you find yourself at the wrong end of a rifle. Sometimes a
fellow must kill or be killed."

Edward had always tried to do what he believed was
right. It wasn't always easy, even in time of peace. Now war
had been declared. The country was calling her boys to fight
the enemy. Edward thought of his friends who would be re-
ceiving their uniforms and sailing for the battlefields of
France. They weren't afraid to go where there was danger.
What would they think of him if he stayed at home! A
shirker! A coward! That's what they would say.

Edward knew then how a fellow feels when he meets a
crisis in his life. Being a Christian meant a decision either for
Christ or for himself. Suddenly Edward knew.

"My friends are ready to face death because they think
that is the way to conquer the enemy. If I want to conquer
the enemy my way I must be ready to face death too. I will
serve with friendliness and not with force. I will save life instead of destroying it. I'll find some place where I can serve
as a Christian even though it may be a very dangerous
place."

After Edward had decided what he wanted to do he acted immediately. He had a friend who knew what was happening in many parts of the world. Surely he would know of a place where people were hungry or lonely and needed help. Over the telephone Edward explained what he wanted and the voice of his friend answered:

"Go to northwest Persia. For two years armies have been fighting across the plains, ruining the crops, and leaving thousands of people homeless. Other Americans have already gone to Persia to take food to the starving people. You could go, too, and work for American Relief."

"That sounds like the place for me."

"But Persia isn't a very safe place to be just now. Russians and Turks and Armenians are all trying to get control of the country. Up in the highlands gangs of thieves are running wild. Besides that, smallpox and typhoid are killing hundreds in the cities," Edward's friend warned.

"I don't *want* an easy job. The boys in the army are ready to go to dangerous places and I am, too. I want to go where I can save someone's life," replied Edward.

Within a month Edward was on his way to Persia. When he arrived at Urumiah (U-rū-mī′a), a Persian city close to the Turkish border, he found everything to be true that his friend had said. The dingy clay-built houses and dusty courtyards of Urumiah were filled with people without homes. Filth and flies were everywhere. People were continually quarreling in the narrow, evil-smelling streets and alleyways.

"Yes," thought Edward, "Persia is the place for me."

Other American relief workers were already busy helping the poor people of Urumiah and the peasants in the near-by villages. Edward went to work at once where help was needed most. First he gave food and clothing to the children whose parents were killed when the soldiers came marching through.

His next job was to help the women whose homes were destroyed during the war. Soon hundreds of homeless women were once again busy spinning wool and weaving cloth.

Next Edward and his gang of workers cleaned every filthy street and alley, every dusty courtyard packed with refugees. Their work seemed endless.

Meanwhile trouble in the city was growing. The Armenian army now had control of Urumiah. Outside the city the Moslems were gathering their armies, and a large Turkish army was on its way to help the Moslems. The Armenians were thrown into a panic and prepared to escape to the south before the Turks arrived.

News of the coming Turks reached Edward who was stationed with several other Americans at a village two miles from the city. The road that passed their house was the very road on which the Turks would be coming. Should they leave the village with the others who were fleeing? They talked it over and decided to stay.

Later that morning the Turkish army came toward the village. Edward watched the red and white flags come closer and closer. Then, to his horror, he saw that the army was being led by the Kurds, cruel tribesmen from the hill country. What this might mean, he dared not think. But the long line of armed men reached the building and began to file past without stopping.

Suddenly shots rang out from the far side of the compound and through a small back gate came a handful of

stragglers from the main army. A stampede broke out, with shouting and firing on all sides. Edward rushed indoors to join the other Americans and found only the women with their children and the trembling native servants. The only man with them was an invalid and everyone in the house looked to Edward for help.

Just then a violent battering was heard at the outer door. As he went to open it, its panels bulged under the heavy blows of rifle butts. Slipping back the bolt, he flung open the door, crying:

"*Buyurun!*" (Come in!)

Three muzzles pointed at him. Three turbaned Kurds, greed and cruelty written on their dark faces, shouted threateningly at them in Turkish:

"*Pool! Pool!*" (Money! Money!)

"Come," said Edward, and guiding them quickly through the room where his friends were sitting, he led them into the office.

"Look," he said, opening cupboards and drawers for them to ransack.

Then he pointed to the safe that contained relief money. When he went to open it he found it was locked! The man who had the key was gone from the compound.

"The key! Give up the key!" demanded one of the raiders, covering him with a rifle.

Steadily Edward met his eye along the length of the glinting barrel.

"I do not have it. Neither do I know where it is."

Something in his face satisfied the Kurd, and his gun lowered.

"Look," suggested Edward, taking the arm of the raider and pointing to the lock of the safe. "Shoot into it. The lock will spring."

A deafening noise echoed from the courtyard but the lock remained fast. Angrily the three soldiers turned on him. One crashed the butt of his rifle across his shoulder, while another swung a muzzle within six inches of his head.

"You have the key! Give it up, or I will shoot!" shouted the leader.

"I do not have it," said Edward again. "I only wish I could give it to you."

The men hesitated. Then sullenly they drew back, realizing he spoke the truth.

The Kurds helped themselves to a few pieces of clothing but took little of the silver. Finding no other booty they demanded Edward's shoes. He took them off. In a few moments they left; the raid was over! The ruthless Kurds were leaving, almost like gentlemen.

If ye love them which love you, what thank have ye?

If ye do good to them which do good to you, what thank have ye?

But love your enemies . . . and your reward shall be great.

Luke 6:32-35

The Man in the Saffron Robe

The red sun was just setting behind the rugged peaks of the Himalayan mountains in India. Their snow-capped edges were alive with color. The little village of Chakdara (Chāk′där-ä), clinging to the hillside, was ablaze, too. But *it* was ablaze with excitement. Gopal (Gō′pal), the only son of the Rajput (Räj′pōōt), had disappeared. His father had not discovered his absence until evening because he thought he was tending the goats on the hillside.

For months there had been trouble in Gopal's family because he was a Christian. This seemed like a terrible disgrace to the proud father. He was a Rajput, a member of the ruling and fighting caste of India. Surely it couldn't be that his son had become a Christian. The landowner beat his son. He starved him. But Gopal would not change his mind. And now—now he was gone!

Samuel Stokes, the American, was gone too. He had given all his possessions to the poor so he could be a *sadhu* (sä′dōō) or holy man. After three days of prayer he had put on the saffron yellow robe worn by the sadhus. He knew the Indians would listen to a sadhu when they would not listen to an American *sahib* (sä′ĭb) or boss. Samuel Stokes loved his Indian friends and he wanted them to know his Saviour.

"The American sadhu is gone and my son is gone. They must have disappeared together," thundered the Rajput. "We will find them."

The Rajput and a large group of villagers left in the cold still night. They were determined to bring back the boy. But days later the weary hillmen straggled home, bitterly disappointed. They could not find Gopal.

Days passed without news. Weeks stretched into months but still no sign. The Rajput busied himself with his goats and small black oxen, but inside he nursed his anger. He would not forget!

Slowly the winter passed and the streams became swollen with the melting snows. Then news came. A peasant had seen Gopal in a village higher up the valley.

"The Rajput's son is at school in the plains," reported the peasant. "The foreign sadhu himself has baptized him a Christian. They say the boy is an excellent scholar. In four days' time the sadhu comes to Bareri to see his friends at the house of the tea-planter's widow."

The foreign sadhu was coming! It was the Rajput's chance. He could scarcely wait. On the third day he gathered the men of the village and told them his plan.

"We will go to meet the sadhu. By the widow's house we will lie in wait for him. The man who bewitched my son shall die."

At dawn, armed with bamboo poles and knives, the hillmen left Chakdara. Gopal's cousin Ram was among the men as they scrambled down to the river, crossed the swaying bridge above its rushing waters, and climbed swiftly to the opposite slope. Nearing the road by which the sadhu must come, they proceeded cautiously. One man went ahead alone, and then returned to report.

"In the widow's house are two sadhus. One is a foreigner, but not the one we seek. We must wait."

The party hid among the pines below the bungalow. A few yards lower a watchman was stationed to give warning. Hour after hour they waited. The stillness of the mountains was broken only by the sound of the cattle bells among the pines. Dusk fell. Ram was beginning to grow restless when suddenly a dog barked in the distance. The hillmen seized their weapons. The next moment the watchman came running on noiseless feet.

"He is coming!" he whispered.

"Are you sure?" asked the Rajput.

"He is short, barefoot, red-haired. He wears the saffron robe. I tell you, it is he!"

There was a tense pause, then with a wild shout the hillmen attacked. Men dashed from the bungalow. After a few moments of confusion, the hillmen fled, leaving the sadhu on the ground with a terrible wound in his forehead.

Daring as it was, Ram remained behind the rest, determined to learn more about the sadhu. Then he would take word to his uncle, the Rajput. Hiding near the inn he hoped

to overhear the men's talk. His patience was rewarded and this is what he heard:

The police had been informed immediately. The sadhu was not dead. For hours he had lain delirious while his friends nursed him continuously. What most impressed the villagers, however, were the sadhu's words as he regained consciousness.

Over and over again he prayed, "Father, forgive them. . . . Father, forgive them." Then he begged, "Don't tell the police. Don't tell the police."

Ram waited no longer. He must tell his uncle. As fast as he could, he made off through the pine forests, slipping over rocks and steep grassy slopes down to the river. Then up the winding path to Chakdara. But Ram was too late. The police had already raided the village, making many arrests. The Rajput and his men were taken miles away to the prison at Simla.

Snatching a bit of food, Ram was off again. This time he was going to the prison at Simla (Sim'lä). He must know what was happening. He ran along the winding mountain track with the steady loping rhythm of a hillboy. Above him were the brilliant stars. The first golden sunbeams crept over the ridges and down into the deep blue valleys just as he entered Simla. For days Ram haunted the police station, not daring to ask questions. He might be recognized. Somehow he managed to keep himself alive, getting work and food as best he could. One day while he hovered outside the court-room, the door opened and out walked the Rajput and his men. They were free! As they took the road which led to Chakdara, they told Ram their story.

"The sadhu himself pleaded for us. Unable to walk, he was carried by litter from Bareri. Fifty miles! He saw the deputy commissioner not once or twice, but many times. And now we are free. The deputy commissioner was angry and threatened us, but he released us, every one."

That night the village buzzed with talk. Why had the sadhu risked his life to plead for the men who tried to kill him? Why did Gopal want to leave them to become a Christian? No one could give the answers.

Years passed. One day Gopal and the sadhu returned to Chakdara. Again the village was ablaze with excitement but this time there was rejoicing in Gopal's home. Now the Rajput and the hillmen were eager to listen to the sadhu as he told them about his Saviour. The good news spread quickly and it was not long until the whole village had heard about the Master.

If ye love me keep my commandments.

JOHN 14:15

The Price of Loyalty

The early Christians were strange people—at least to the eyes of their heathen neighbors. They refused to go to pagan hospitals because the priests walked through the rooms among the sick people chanting to some heathen god. They refused to go to gladiatorial combats to see men kill each other or to the theater to watch the cruel, coarse plays.

But strangest of all was their zeal for telling others about Jesus. Missionaries walked long distances to tell people in faraway towns and villages that Jesus died for their sins. Men preached powerful sermons in market places and synagogues and wrote appealing letters to faraway friends. In every city where Christians lived, they told their neighbors about Jesus, the Son of God and the Saviour of the world.

Soon people all over the world knew the good news, although many of them did not accept it.

Some who thought their ways were strange became their enemies. They persecuted the Christians for obeying Christ. They put some in prison; some they tied to stakes and burned to death; others they threw to the lions. In spite of this persecution, more and more people learned to love Jesus until there were Christians in Jerusalem and Rome, Spain and Africa.

The story of the Saviour found its way to the little coun-

try of Numidia in Africa, where a young man named Maximilian heard it and became a Christian. He, too, read what Jesus said about loving and hating, doing good and forgiving.

"If I love God," thought Maximilian, "then I will do what He says."

In A.D. 295, when Maximilian was twenty-one, the recruiting officer in Numidia came looking for strong young men to fill in the ranks of the Roman army. He needed men who would become expert swordsmen and javelin throwers. Maximilian was one of those chosen to drill and train and serve in the Roman army for twenty years.

The young men were taken before the proconsul of Africa to be examined. Maximilian stood before the big official, Dion, and bravely told him he could not serve in the army nor wear a soldier's badge. "I cannot do it because I am a Christian," he explained.

Dion tried again and again to persuade him to serve, but Maximilian always replied, "I serve Christ."

At last Dion said, "But in the armies of our lords who rule Rome there are Christian soldiers and they serve."

"They know what is fitting for them; but I know what Christ wants me to do," Maximilian said firmly.

When the proconsul saw that nothing could be done to sway Maximilian, he stopped trying to persuade him. Maximilian was condemned to die. At the age of twenty-one they cut off his head for refusing to serve in the Roman army. In Carthage they buried him.

The officers of the Roman army did not know that Maximilian was already serving One great leader, Jesus Christ, and that loyalty to Jesus was worth more than his own life.

If he repent, forgive him.

LUKE 17:3

Pastor John

Acres of Montana wheat stretched out like a soft green carpet on either side of the road that led to the Independence School. Large, well-kept farms with clean fence rows and herds of sleek cattle gave the Yellowstone Valley an air of prosperity. The center of activities for this Bloomfield settlement was the Bethlehem Mennonite Church, where the people met week after week for worship.

But the days of World War I brought sadness to many homes in the settlement: the sadness that comes from being misunderstood by neighbors; the sadness that comes when families are separated. The Mennonites' refusal to take part in war was considered foolish and unpatriotic by those who did not understand what God teaches about killing and war.

No doubt Pastor John Franz was thinking of his troubled

friends as he and his family drove toward the schoolhouse just a mile from their home. Untiringly he had visited those who needed encouragement and represented his men before draft boards when misunderstandings developed. He little suspected that soon he would need their help.

"It is nearly time for the meeting to begin," he said to his wife as they approached the schoolhouse. "I'll get the mail before we go in." Their mailbox stood across the road from the schoolhouse.

Glancing through the papers, he found that his copy of the *Mountain Lake Observer* had come. He enjoyed reading this paper with its pages of German news and the daily happenings of Mountain Lake, for Mountain Lake, Minnesota, had been his home town when he was a boy. In this community John's German grandparents settled after leaving their home in Russia. Here, too, John was born.

But he had no time for reading now. He must hurry to the meeting, for matters of school business were to be discussed with the parents of the Independence School children.

As they entered the school grounds John noticed two strange cars parked near the road. He wondered a little why strangers had come to the meeting, but there was no time to talk as they hurried toward the little white frame building. Scarcely had they taken their seats in the crowded room when the meeting was called to order.

Meanwhile, unnoticed by John, one of the strangers slipped into the room. Glancing quickly through the group he located the man he wanted. He approached John, and asked him to step outside the building for a few minutes. John gathered up his mail as he followed, wondering what the man could want.

No sooner was he outside the building than a group of rough men appeared, demanding that he follow them to the car. When John stopped to question their sudden action, several of the men grabbed him and dragged him to one of the cars that was parked near the road, ready to leave.

The men would give no reason for their sudden action other than the short reply, "You have a German paper with you. You are the man who is making all this trouble."

Feeling against Germany ran high during the war months. Many of these Mennonites spoke the German language and were born of German-speaking parents. This, added to the fact that they were conscientious objectors, caused people to treat them unkindly.

By this time Mrs. Franz and others in the meeting noticed that something unusual was happening outside. She hurried out to the car.

"What are you going to do with my husband?" she cried.

"It's none of your business! We're only taking him for a ride," the men shouted as they knocked her to the ground. She lay there unconscious. The men drove away quickly.

John barely noticed the familiar surroundings as they sped down the country roads. He was thinking, "Where can they be taking me? What could they plan to do?" The answer to these questions lay on the floor of the car. Guns, shovels, and a rope spoke grimly of what awaited him at the end of his ride.

Before long the familiar scenes of Bloomfield were exchanged for the less familiar Bad Lands. Usually John enjoyed the quaint peaks and oddly shaped pinnacles that the winds and rains of centuries had carved into the sandstone. When he looked at them against the clear Montana sky, their colors of red and brown and purple were satisfying and restful. Now concern for his wife's welfare and fear of what lay before him made them appear weird and grotesque.

When the car stopped beside a large tree John fully realized what the men planned to do. He watched them quietly as they fastened the rope to an overhanging branch. If his spirit sank within him as the men argued noisily among themselves, he gave no sign. They were nearly finished now. This minute might be his last!

"Lord, I belong to you," he prayed. "Your will be done— Your will be done."

He let them take him roughly to the tree where the noose hung ready. Then he noticed the county sheriff and district attorney in the group. Seeing an opportunity he spoke.

"I am an American citizen. My father was an American citizen and my grandfather was a naturalized citizen. If you kill me you will be murderers. Think of that!"

They stopped, while the sheriff, afraid of what might happen if they hanged John, persuaded the drunken men to turn him over to the Glendive Jail. But the men plotted among themselves to return late that evening and hang him from a bridge over the Yellowstone River.

Meanwhile the news of what had happened at the schoolhouse spread throughout the community. The members of the church gathered together. While they were praying for their pastor, some of the leaders met with Mrs. Franz. They decided to take her and the boys to the sheriff's office at the Glendive County Jail. Surely he could help them. After a two-hour trip over rugged roads they arrived at the jail. They knocked persistently and a man opened the door.

"Well, what do you want, lady?" he asked abruptly.

"I'd like to see the sheriff," replied Mrs. Franz.

"Sorry, he's not here. Maybe he's out of town. I don't know," he said gruffly.

As Mrs. Franz turned to leave, a side door suddenly opened. There stood the sheriff!

Fear seized Mrs. Franz. She had seen this man before. He—why he was one of the men who kidnaped her husband!

"What have you done with John?" she cried.

"I don't know what you're talking about," the sheriff answered.

"That can't be true. You were at the Independence School this afternoon," Mrs. Franz said.

"Oh, yes, I remember," the sheriff spoke awkwardly.

"Where is he? What have you done to him?"

"Come back in half an hour. You may see him then," the sheriff agreed reluctantly.

Mrs. Franz and the boys waited anxiously while the thirty minutes dragged by. Then once more they knocked at the sheriff's door. After persistent knocking they were allowed to enter. There, behind locked doors she found her husband. What a change had taken place in him! Lines of care were written deep in his face. He looked years older. Kneeling together in the sheriff's office, the family prayed earnestly to God for help and protection.

When the sheriff returned to dismiss the visitors, John insisted that they stay. Women had never been allowed to stay with their prisoner husbands before, but since his wife was not well, John begged the sheriff for this one consideration. Reluctantly the sheriff gave him a private room in the jail where the family could sleep that night. In the daytime they were forced to leave.

The next day was Sunday, and so nothing happened, but on Monday evening a crowd began to gather at the city hall. Mrs. Franz wondered what it could mean. They heard footsteps in the corridor; then John was taken from the room.

Late that evening John told his wife what had happened in the courtroom.

"During the trial they hurled questions at me from all sides," he began. " 'Are you a citizen? Do you speak German? Is it true you have a German paper?' "

"Finally they asked, 'Why do you and your people refuse

to buy war bonds?' I tried to explain simply that Christians really own nothing. We are here to take care of all God's things. Since our money is God's money, we can use it only for things that please Him. We canot buy war bonds, because that makes war possible. Using our money to make it possible for others to be killed would be just as wrong as going into the army and killing a man ourselves."

"And did you explain what we gladly do instead?" asked Mrs. Franz.

"Yes, I told them our community gave twice as much food and clothing for refugees as any other community of its size in the state. They seemed surprised."

"And what are they planning to do now?" asked Mrs. Franz anxiously.

"I don't know. We can only wait and see."

Three days later, the county officials released John under $3,000 bond. They felt sure the money could not be raised. As soon as John's church heard this story, its leaders met again. In three hours they had the papers arranged and the $3,000 ready.

The county authorities were amazed. Why would these people trust their leader so completely? John said the truth when he told them, "Our church is a brotherhood. When someone is in need we help him in a spirit of Christian love."

The family returned home but John was told to report to Glendive each month to answer questions that might come up. Before the end of the first month the money was returned and John received a letter that said:

"You do not need to come to Glendive to answer questions."

The war ended and the trouble seemed to be forgotten.

Later, friends on the edge of the Mennonite settlement learned that the county officers had heard false stories about the Mennonites. Important lawyers talked with John many times and urged him to sue the officers and wealthy businessmen in court. They knew these men had done wrong. But John always said:

"It is not my business to get even. The Bible says, 'Vengeance is mine; I will repay, saith the Lord.' I'll leave it to Him."

One day several years later as John and his son Rufus were cutting grain, a car stopped beside the field and the driver came toward them.

"Do you know me, Mr. Franz?" the man asked as he approached.

"Why, yes, I do. How could I forget you? You were one of the twelve men who tried to hang me!"

"Yes," he answered, soberly. "I have come to ask a hard thing of you. Will you forgive me for the great wrong I did to you and to your family?"

Suddenly the fields seemed very quiet. John remembered: the two strange cars, a rope, a lonely tree, bleak walls of a prison cell, a court room. Could he forgive? John reached out his hand with a smile.

"I forgive you from my heart," he said.

Blessed are the merciful.

Jacob Decides

The young people of the Amish settlement at Northkill had returned to their homes from the apple-snitzing and frolic at Jacob Hochstetler's. It was late. The cabin was quiet and Jacob Hochstetler and his family had retired for the night.

The settlers often recalled the days in the old country and no doubt Jacob was also thinking of the comforts of his home in Europe before he dropped off to sleep. Many people had left Switzerland and the Palatinate to find a home in America where they could worship God as they wished.

One day Jacob selected the land on which they were to build their new home. He knew good farm land when he saw it and the acres that he chose had not one waste field. Besides, the rapidly flowing Northkill Creek that lay just to the

41

west promised a constant source of water power. Jacob had made a wise choice.

The Northkill settlement was new (established around 1739), and the few families living at the edge of the frontier were far from the protection of the older colonies. Jacob and his friends were among the first to cross the Blue Mountains to settle near what is now Harrisburg, Pennsylvania.

At first they had no trouble with the Indians because they treated them fairly. Indians frequently visited the settlers. The newcomers and the Indians lived together in peace.

However, in 1754 an unfortunate thing happened. Both

the French and the English were settling in the New World and both wanted to be the rulers of the country. This led to the French and Indian War, with the Indians helping the French fight the English. As a result of this war, the Indians broke friendship with the settlers and staged massacres on the frontier colonists. The once peaceful settlement along the Northkill now lived in daily fear of an attack.

All during the summer months of 1754, the Amish families had very few gatherings because they feared a surprise attack by the Indians. But as September drew near, and disturbances became fewer, they again visited their friends. Since they were scattered and few in number, they enjoyed these gatherings even more after the long weeks of separation. The evening with the Hochstetler family had been a happy one.

Now they were sound asleep. Even the dog was in his usual corner near the blackened hearth. Suddenly he raised his head, his ears standing at attention. He growled strangely at the sounds that came from the yard, awakening young Jacob who slept near by. Sensing that something was amiss, Jacob opened the door to see what could be the matter. Suddenly a shot rang out. Streaks of pain pierced his leg.

In an instant the entire family was out of bed. Peering through the windows, they could make out the figures of eight or ten Indians standing in consultation near the bake oven. Quickly Joseph and Christian reached for their guns.

But father intervened. "No, no, boys," he said.

"But Father," the boys begged, "you can't let us die when we could save ourselves." The boys, like their father, were good steady marksmen, and they felt sure they could save the family.

This was an hour of severe trial for the father who dearly loved his family. Should he kill the Indians and save his family? Surely this would be a father's duty.

But the firm conviction of years held true. To kill was sin—even in self-defense. He could not kill these Indians and still obey Christ's command of love.

And if they murdered his family? No doubt Jacob would have said, "Then I will have done what is right and if God wants to take us home to heaven that is where we will want to be."

When he thought about it this way it was not difficult for him to say to his boys, "It would never be right to take the life of another even to save one's own. We will not shoot the Indians."

But there was no time to think of these things now. The Indians were already setting fire to the buildings. Flames crackled and the acrid smell of smoke filtered into the cabin. Before long the fierce heat of the fire drove the four children and their parents to the refuge of the cellar. Outside, the Indians stood guard in silent expectancy.

Streaks of light began to show in the east. "If we can hold out until daylight, the Indians may leave," thought Jacob. Determinedly he and the boys beat back the flames as they burst through the floor. For a time they poured cider on the flames, but that was soon gone.

The Indians became uneasy as the streaks in the sky widened into broad bands of light. Before long the painted figures began to disappear one by one into the shadows at the edge of the clearing.

Inside the flaming house the heat was nearly unbearable. When Jacob observed the Indians' retreat he said, "Quick!

They're leaving! We can get out through this window."

Mrs. Hochstetler was a heavy woman. After persistent effort she managed to crawl out through the narrow window. Jacob, too, needed help because of his wounded leg. Christian and Joseph, with their sister and father, made their escape easily.

Unknown to the fleeing family, one young brave had lingered behind to gather ripe peaches. He saw them and gave the alarm. By the time they were all out of the crumbling cabin, the Indians were back and easily captured them.

In the meantime the neighbors to the west heard the disturbance and running through the woods to the edge of the meadow, came upon the Indians. Horrified, they saw that young Jacob, Mrs. Hochstetler, and her daughter were all dead. The bloody work was done. The Indians took Jacob and his two sons, Joseph and Christian, and silently disappeared into the forest.

Several days later in Philadelphia, Christopher Sauer published an account of the massacres in his German paper:

"I am sorry that I cannot send you better news, as the Indians have again murdered many inhabitants beyond us. . . . The poor people beyond us will all be obliged to move away. We stand in great fear. Yesterday we heard all day long of murder and death. No one, however, is ready to oppose the enemy."

Pray for them which despitefully use you.

MATTHEW 5:44

On Corridor Two

"Ernest Swalm?" asked the Major as Ernie entered the room.

"Yes, sir."

"You refuse to put on your uniform?"

"Yes, sir. I am a Christian. I cannot kill my enemies, for the Scriptures say, 'Love your enemies.' Nor can I wear the uniform of an organization whose business it is to kill."

"You conscientious objectors used to be excused when the other boys were drafted," the Major said. "Now our Canadian Parliament has passed a bill that says you must serve as noncombatants. We will give you a job where you won't need to kill anyone. You can be a stretcher bearer and help the wounded soldiers. You would really be doing good then."

"Thank you, sir, but I cannot serve in the army, no matter what the job is. I'd still be a part of the army, and its purpose is to kill. I would gladly take care of wounded people, but not as a member of the army."

"And I suppose you have some Scripture for that too?" scoffed the Major.

"Yes," Ernie replied. "Saul of Tarsus was a noncombatant. He only *held* the clothes of those who stoned Stephen. The Bible doesn't say he threw any stones, yet he was just as guilty of the crime as those who really killed him. He consented to Stephen's death. That is why I can't take any of the jobs in the army. They are all part of a plan to kill men. And, as a Christian, I cannot kill."

Not long after this, Ernest Swalm was court-martialed and sentenced to two years of hard labor for refusing military service during World War I.

He, with other conscientious objectors from many different denominations (Ernie was a member of the Brethren in Christ Church of Canada), was taken to the Lincoln County Jail. The boys were to stay at this jail until the provincial sheriff came to take them to the federal prison at Kingston.

They were searched when they arrived. Everything was taken from them except their Bibles. Then they were given jail uniforms and sent to their cells. Ernie's cell was number twenty-three.

Ernie slept soundly that night. Next morning he did not awaken until the sun was high in the sky. He lay there, staring at the narrow cell of whitewashed brick. It was a little room, with not even one nail on which to hang his coat —only the grim iron gates in front.

"I could be out with the rest of the boys if I'd only serve

in the army," Ernie thought. "I wonder if I'm being foolish . . . ?"

Just then, the lines of an old hymn came to him:

"But prisons would palaces prove
If Jesus would dwell with me there."

During the four weeks that followed, Ernie discovered the truth of those words. Christ became real to him in a new way. He had so much time, he could spend hours in Bible study and prayer.

The turnkey of the jail was Garley Clinch, a man nearly seventy years old. He hated conscientious objectors and did all he could to make them miserable. He became angry when the men prayed and sang hymns, and sometimes ordered them to stop. Ernie decided to pray for him every day.

Several days later another conscientious objector was brought to jail from camp, and Garley turned him in.

"Here, boys," he said, "I brought one of your pals. I think when I'm good enough to do that, you ought to sing a hymn for me."

The men were surprised to hear this from one who had been so bitter, but before long corridor two echoed with:

"How good is the God we adore,
Our faithful, unchangeable friend.
His love is as great as His power
And knows neither measure nor end."

The boys stopped after one stanza, but Garley said, "Please sing another." By the time they finished, tears were trickling down his face.

"Thank you, boys," he said. The big iron gates clanged shut behind him.

The men could see that Garley's heart was softening. Early each morning they gathered together in one of the cells to pray for him. They knew that even a man seventy years old could be saved.

From that time on Garley was a real friend. Instead of persecuting the boys, he granted them many kind favors.

One Monday morning four weeks after Ernie's arrival at the jail, Garley came to his cell and said, "You're wanted in the office." Leading the way to the dressing room he added, "Your release came through this morning."

Then the boys learned that the Canadian government was again excusing Christian conscientious objectors from army service. They would not need to fight. They could go home! Garley told them the good news.

"Thank you for your kindness during these hard weeks," Ernie said as he gave good-by to the old turnkey.

"Don't thank me. I'm ashamed of the way I treated you when you first came. I've never had a set of prisoners like you boys before."

"When the letter came saying I had to go to camp, I was very unhappy," Ernie said, "but now I'm glad I was sent to jail. Right here on corridor two I learned to love Jesus better than ever before. I had plenty of time to talk to Him. I'll be praying for you, Garley."

Fifteen years passed. Ernest Swalm was holding tent meetings in Elgin County, Ontario. Just as he was ready to close, he noticed two men coming into the tent. One of them was Allen Morrison, his cell mate of number twenty-three. After the service, Ernest rushed out to greet his old friend. He hadn't seen Allen since the day they said good-by on corridor two of the Lincoln County Jail.

"And did you hear that old Garley Clinch became a Christian before I left the jail?" continued Allen as they recalled their experiences of the past years.

"Yes, I heard," Ernest replied. "Tell me more about it."

"One day after the other boys had gone home, Garley asked me to pray with him," Allen explained. "I had the happy privilege of leading him to Christ. That fall, during a Spanish influenza epidemic, Garley took sick and died. He was anxious to go to his Lord. His last words were, 'I'm so glad I met the conscientious objectors. They meant so much to me.'"

"But I must tell you one more thing," Allen went on.

"Shortly before he took sick, he brought me an old Bible and said, 'Allen, I want to give you the Clinch family Bible. It's been in our family for a hundred years. You've meant more to me than any of my relatives, so I want you to have it.' "

"You can imagine how happy I was for that, Ernest. And whenever I look at it I remember how learning to love Christ changed Garley."

Do good to them that hate you.

MATTHEW 5:44

The Mystery of the Thatch

If Preacher Peter had been awake, he would have heard their quick footsteps as the shadowy figures of the young men made their way down the cobblestone street of the little village in the Emmenthal, Switzerland.

Each step brought the young men closer and closer to the darkened home of the old Mennonite minister and his wife. Life for them had been very difficult for they lived in the eighteenth century when Mennonites were still being persecuted in Switzerland.

"Now we will see what kind of a man he is," muttered one of the young men. "Maybe he won't be so loving after our visit tonight!" he laughed.

"That is the house," whispered another as they slackened

their pace. Cautiously they approached the darkened dwelling while their eyes searched the darkness.

"No one is stirring. Let us do our job well."

The men quickly lifted themselves to the roof and soon the muffled sound of falling thatch blended in with other night sounds. They worked quickly lest someone should surprise them in their treachery.

Inside Peter stirred in his sleep. The strange sounds continued and Peter sat up in his bed.

"Something is not right," thought Peter. "There are noises on the roof."

Carefully he made his way across the bedroom floor, through the darkened room, and reaching the outside doorway he quietly opened the latch. Peering cautiously into the night he could make out the figures of several men busily at work.

"What can this mean!" he gasped, as he stared in amazement. "Destroying my thatch!"

Slowly the meaning of their actions became clear to him. He knew that many people in the Emmenthal did not understand why he and his people believed it was wrong to go to war. When they had been threatened with imprisonment and death, Peter and his friends would simply say, "We would rather die the bitterest death than disobey God."

"Now they have come to molest me again," thought Peter.

Raising his eyes heavenward, Peter prayed God to help him do what was right. Then turning, he walked quickly into the little house.

"Mother," he called, "workmen have come to us; you had better prepare a meal."

The strange happenings of the past few minutes had startled his wife, but now she understood. Soon she was busily at work in the little kitchen. And before long a meal was waiting on the neatly spread table.

Opening the door once more, the aged minister called to the boys on the roof, "You have worked long and hard. Surely you are hungry. Now come in to us and eat."

Hesitatingly they came into the room and stood awkwardly around the table where the lighted tapers gave the room a friendly glow. Peter urged them to be seated and finally they found their places where they sat uncomfortably, staring at their plates.

Peter bowed his head and folded his hands while the guests sat in silence. Then in his kindly voice, Peter prayed earnestly and fervently and lovingly for the guests and for his family. When the last words of the kindly prayer were spoken, the young men raised faces flushed with shame. The food was passed and found its way on to their plates, but it seemed they could not eat. Each sat silent before his well-filled plate.

Suddenly, as if by signal, the men pushed back their chairs and quickly disappeared through the door which they had entered moments before. Once again there were footsteps on the roof, and the shuffle of thatch could be heard. But this time it was not the sound of falling thatch. They were putting it back on the roof! Then, if Preacher Peter were listening (and I think he was), he would have heard the running footsteps of his guests as they disappeared down the cobblestone street and into the night.

Do good, and lend, hoping for nothing again; . . . and ye shall be the children of the Highest.

LUKE 6:35

The Pick and Shovel Army

Thoughtfully, the bronzed muscular giant in blue overalls and hobnailed boots listened to the mayor's story as they stood together on the heap of fallen brick.

"That night one hundred and two houses were destroyed here in Lagarde," the mayor said sadly. "Only eighteen are left. Village after village went under as the waters of the Tarn River overflowed its banks. Most of the people who were saved from the rushing waters are homeless. We are grateful for the food and money sent from all over France, but now we need help to rebuild our homes and clear the fields. Pierre, I know what your army did two years ago when floods covered parts of Lichtenstein (Lĭk′tĕn-shtīn). Will you come to Lagarde (Lä-gärd′)?"

Pierre Ceresole (Py-ĕr′ Sĕr′ĕ-zôl) looked at the empty

shells—once cozy homes—and their perilously leaning walls. He saw the fields covered with piles of rubbish.

"It will be dangerous work," the mayor went on. "Can you pull down those walls and remake roads?"

"We will do what we can," Pierre said. "I do not know how many volunteers will come, but I will send out the call."

"There is no money to pay you," the mayor reminded him.

"We work without pay," Pierre replied. "Can you give us food and lodging?"

"There is the old chateau." The mayor pointed to an empty house undamaged by the flood. "And the commune (cŏm'yūn) will allow you money for food."

Immediately Pierre sent out a call for volunteers. They came—tramping, cycling, motoring, or by train. Before long the streets of Lagarde echoed with shouts and greetings in many languages. There were forty-two workers from Switzerland, Russia, Germany, America, England, and India. Many more would have come, but there was no more room at the chateau.

The idea for Pierre's peace army began to grow while he was a young man in Switzerland. Switzerland required all of its strong young men to train for military service. Some of them believed military training was always wrong, but they wanted to serve their country in some good way. So in 1920 Pierre and his friends organized an army that they called The International Voluntary Civilian Service. Men and even women from other countries joined the volunteers to help wherever they were needed. Each summer, during vacation time, they built bridges, cleared flood lands, and rebuilt homes. This was their way of helping their country.

When the peace army arrived at Lagarde, the men lost no time in getting to work. At half past four every morning reveille sounded. By five o'clock breakfast was served. And at half past five, everybody trooped out to work. By the time the village stirred from its sleep, the pick and shovel army was already hard at work.

The people of Lagarde were astonished as they watched them work: miners, masons, doctors, lawyers, musicians, and students, side by side. The schoolteachers, nurses, dressmakers, and typists were busy at the chateau cooking, washing, scrubbing, and sewing for the men.

At the end of the long day, weary in every muscle and streaked with dust and perspiration, the workers hurried for a shower or a dip in the river. Then came supper, followed by a sing. Each worker sang the songs of his own nation and the countryside rang with the sound.

Weeks went by. Under Pierre's leadership, in scorching sun or drizzling rain the men climbed the walls of ruined buildings and girdled them with ropes. Then they began the dangerous tug of war which ended in a crash of bricks and clouds of choking dust. They shifted fallen trees and piles of rubbish. They remade roads and paths.

All through the summer they worked. When the job was finished Pierre was able to return to the poor little town seventeen thousand francs ($800) of the food money the mayor had given him.

On the last evening the grateful people of Lagarde gathered on the chateau grounds to say good-by to their guests. As the mayor rose to thank Pierre Ceresole and his army, the crowd grew very quiet.

"After you have gone," he said, "your spirit of love will

still remain. You have made us see that nations can help each other. You have made us want to help others. For this whole village I say, 'Thank you.' "

A loud cheer broke the stillness of the evening air. Then the people of Lagarde and the tired volunteers from all over the world joined in singing their songs together for the last time. By morning the pick and shovel army had gone.

Flood and storm and landslide were the enemies the pick and shovel army fought each following year. In 1931 they were called to fight a new enemy at Brynmawr, a little town in Wales. The men of Brynmawr had been out of work for years. Their wives and children often went hungry and some wore only rags. But a few of them could not sit at home and do nothing. They decided to fill their empty days with work for their own town. They started to clear away the huge rubbish heap with its old tin cans and broken bottles, and the ugly coal dumps, and to build playgrounds and gardens, a swimming pool, and a wading pool for the children.

Week after week, month after month went by. These men worked untiringly for over two years! During the second summer Pierre heard of the poor little mining town and the hardworking men. Again he sounded the call and soon men and women from all over Europe were coming to Brynmawr.

In the days that followed, the people of Brynmawr saw that Pierre's army worked for peace and happiness instead of destruction. Gladly the miners showed the less experienced newcomers how to use a pick and shovel. In the evening when the day's work was done everyone shared in singing or hiking or talking.

One day a letter came for Pierre. The postmark was Lagarde! As he read the note enclosed, a smile broke over his face—then tears came to his eyes. Turning to his friends crowded around him, he said,

"You remember the seventeen thousand francs we returned to the people of Lagarde? They needed every *sou* (sōō) of it. Yet listen to this:

" 'To help you to continue with your useful work as in the past and to crown your patient efforts with prompt success, the Commune of Lagarde sends you the money you returned to us. Good courage, friends, we are with you. You can count on us.' "

The victims of the flood in southern France had sent

nearly eight hundred dollars to help the poor people of Brynmawr!

Steadily the work went forward. Good progress had been made when the pick and shovel army left in October. All through the autumn, winter, and spring the miners continued to work, until the peace army returned the following summer. At last both the swimming pool and wading pool were ready for use. Pierre stood where the old coal dump had blackened the ground not long before. Now he saw a park, ablaze with thousands of poppies, rich green grass, and winding paths. The houses had been whitewashed and gardens were gay with flowers. From the wading pool he heard the sound of children shouting at play. A new spirit was abroad in Brynmawr.

"Best payday I ever had was when I saw those children splash in the pool for the first time," said one of the fathers, turning to Pierre. "If the entrance money taken at the swimming pool more than covers the cost, I reckon we ought to send what's left to help some other place build one."

On the day of the official opening every man, woman, and child of the neighborhood was there. Even the mayor of Lagarde was invited for the occasion. The happy crowd grew quiet as he started to speak—he spoke in French, with Pierre at his elbow, translating.

"When our country was flooded, Pierre Ceresole and his peace army came to our rescue. We wanted to pass on this kindness to others. We heard of the distress here in Brynmawr and sent you seventeen thousand francs. If our governments would spend money helping each other in this way we would all become good friends."

Ye are my disciples, if ye have love one to another.

JOHN 13:35

Peter's Plea

"Bring me my clothes, Susanna," Peter called weakly as he pulled himself to a sitting position on the edge of his bed. "I am going to the market place."

"To the market place!" cried his wife. "Why, Peter, you can't possibly think of leaving the house with such a high fever. You know it has been weeks since you have been well."

"But I must go!" Peter replied firmly. "Last night sleep would not come for I could not forget about the sadness of our Jewish neighbors. While I lay awake with their trouble heavy on my heart, the Lord spoke to me. He wants me to help them. That is why I must go to the market place."

Susanna knew Peter had been following the papers carefully these past weeks. She had seen his mounting concern and restlessness as he read how thousands of Jews were being massacred in the larger cities. A riot had taken place in their own town of Sevastopol. Hundreds of Jews lived in Sevastopol, and Peter Friesen knew their lives were no longer safe.

When the Russian government plunged the country into war against Japan in 1904 the people were distressed. They did not want the troubles that come with war. Their resentment became so strong that the government officials saw they must do something to turn the people's attention from the war, or else there would be an uprising.

"If we can only make it look like the Jews caused this trouble, the people will hate them instead of us," they thought.

Secretly they plotted with rioters in many towns. Men who already disliked the Jews were only too glad to help in their terrible plan. Now the troublemakers had come to Sevastopol.

Susanna knew that her warmhearted husband would do all in his power to help these hunted people. She thought of the many who came to their home for help and comfort. They were never turned away until they had received the kindness and understanding that only Peter could give. But this time Susanna feared for the safety of her husband. An angry mob was nothing to be trifled with. Tearfully she begged Peter to give up his plan.

"I must go," he replied.

Peter knew that the mob would be restless and that tempers would be running high as the speakers called out hateful lies against their Jewish neighbors. He knew that he would be hated—yes, and perhaps killed—for defending these helpless people.

Peter knew even more that he must go.

The two knelt at their bedside for nearly an hour, calling for the help and blessing of their heavenly Father. Peter's heart poured out its heavy load of sadness for the terribly mistreated people.

Then slowly he made his way to the door and out onto the street. Susanna watched her husband as he almost staggered down the street toward the angry rioters. Anxiously she breathed a prayer for his safety.

As Peter neared the market place he quickened his steps. He did not hear the familiar calls of the merchants from their stalls nor the bargaining of the traders. Instead there was the sound of angry voices and above the noise of the crowd came sharp and angry words. At the turn of the street he came upon them—that great angry mob of workmen.

Peter pressed his way through the great pushing throng to a wagon that had been surrounded by the people. As his full voice carried across the market place the sea of angry men quieted. Peter's sickness and weakness were gone and with pleading in his voice he called out to the crowd below:

"You call yourselves Christian, and that you are since you believe in Christ. But let us remember that Christ loved all men and even died for them.

"Through His death all men became brothers, and brothers do not kill each other. They love each other. You remember how Cain killed his brother, but there is not one here in this crowd that would want to dirty his hands with his brother's blood."

He continued to plead with the attentive crowd for nearly an hour. Then as they waited expectantly, he leaned over the edge of the wagon and pulled a large Russian to his side.

"You are my brother," he cried as he kissed the rough, dirty face of the workman. "Now we will all go home and to our work."

A strange hush hung over the crowd as Peter's last words carried out to those along the edges. He stood silent, not knowing what the men would do next. Then one by one they slipped away from the crowd and disappeared down the street.

Soon Peter was alone and very tired. Wearily he stumbled home to bed. The fever returned but no Jew was hurt in Sevastopol.

Blessed are the peacemakers: for they shall be called the children of God.

MATTHEW 5:9

The Peacemaker

Risku (Risk'ōō) hoisted himself to the top of the narrow mud wall. Risku was an expert builder of little African mud huts with cone-shaped grass roofs and open doorways. No one in the little village of Garkida (Gaar'kĭd-daah) could make better and stronger huts than his. He had already built three huts for the missionaries, but since they needed six more, he and his native friends continued to work busily. As the men worked they watched these strangers. Someone had warned them that white men beat their native workers. But the days passed one by one and Risku and his friends did not see one white man beating a native.

Risku thought to himself, "These missionaries aren't like other white people. I will watch them closely."

But the missionaries were also watching Risku. They saw

how carefully he shaped the mud walls and filled the cracks until they were smooth and firm. They saw how he wove long grasses into a tight thick rope, placed it along the top of the mud wall, and laid the grass roof. They saw how kind he was to his African friends.

"Risku would make a fine worker for us," they said to each other. "He could help the doctor when he visits the sick people and give out medicine. But . . . . " The words trailed off there. The reason for that "but" was this: Risku was a Mohammedan.

When the doctor asked Risku to help him, Risku did not know what to do.

"I must talk to my teacher first," he told the doctor.

The teacher thought a long time and finally he said, "If I were able to go and work for the white man I would go. I am a Mohammedan teacher, but I'd like to work for these people because they know so much more than I do."

Risku went to the missionary doctor with his answer. After that, he worked faithfully and well. He bandaged ugly sores and gave people medicine. He learned to recognize diseases and to supply the right remedy. Before long, he could help his African friends in many ways.

But Risku did not spend all his time giving out medicine. He noticed that the doctor often read in books. Risku became curious about these books and wished he could learn to read the strange black marks, too. One day the doctor wrote on a piece of paper, *a, e, i, o,* and *u.*

"Learn these letters, Risku, and then I will give you more," he said.

Risku learned all the letters of the alphabet in one day. Soon he learned to read in the little red Bura primer. Finally he was able to read the book of Mark through. Each day as the doctor taught him more about the black marks he would teach him some things about God. Risku thought about the things he was reading and hearing, but he was not sure that they were true. The more he read, the more he began to wonder:

"Is Allah the god I should obey? Is Mohammed really his prophet?"

Then he stopped praying to Mohammed and he stopped fasting during the fast month. He tried to learn more about Jesus. The doctor was happy to teach him about Jesus and how He loves all the people of Africa. It was not long until Risku became a Christian.

Risku continued to help the doctor give out medicine. But he also went from village to village on his bicycle telling his African brothers about the Jesus Road. He was anxious for them to have peace in their hearts, too.

One day visitors from the Church of the Brethren in America came to Africa to visit their mission churches. They worshiped with the Christians in their mud-walled churches and visited them in their little round houses with the pointed grass roofs. Then they started out to visit the Christians in the villages scattered over the whole province. Risku and some of the missionaries went with them. Seven men rode in the little jeep that pulled the trailer which carried their equipment for sleeping.

On the trip home to their own village across the flat, sandy countryside, dotted with rocks and scrubby bushes and trees, the party met an exciting experience. As the travelers rounded a curve in the road, they suddenly came upon a large water hole where wild animals and cattle came to drink. A herd of horned cattle and many natives swarmed around it.

"I believe the people are beginning their harvest feast," the missionary said.

The jeep stopped and the seven men waited to see what would happen. Soon they saw that this was no feast.

"Why, they're quarreling over the water hole!" someone whispered.

In the background were nearly two hundred more men dressed in their fighting clothes, dancing closer and closer to the men defending the water hole. The men in the jeep could see that the warriors were *not* celebrating. Their bodies were decorated with all the *amulets* (am'u-lĕts) they possessed. (Charms put on to protect them from danger.) They carried huge shields and struck the air with their poisoned arrows. Before long the two sides were facing each other, dancing furiously as their arrows and swords cut the air, each waiting for the first arrow to fly.

Risku watched the fighters from the jeep. He had not seen such a battle lately and he had almost forgotten how dangerous they could be. He was fearful for the safety of his missionary friends. As Risku looked more closely he saw that the markings on the men's faces were those of his mother's tribe.

"Why these are the Pulke (Pull'key) men," said Risku. "These are my brothers. I will try to stop them."

The jeep was closest to the warriors defending the water hole, and a few of the more curious ones gathered around the strange-looking car. From some of them Risku soon learned that the men of the neighboring village had claimed

the water and stolen some sheep. Now they were trying to
drive out the Pulke men.

When Risku heard this he was anxious to talk with the
Pulke men. The men in the jeep waited until the warriors
seemed to draw back a little; then they slowly drove across
the lines of armed men. The natives swarmed around the
jeep as Risku began to talk with them in their own dialect.
They told him that the other men had stolen their cattle.

"But fighting is not the way to settle your trouble," said
Risku. "You should let the chief decide."

After pleading with them for a long time Risku turned to one of the leaders and, as was their custom, asked for his left sandal. Holding it high in the air so all could see it, he said,

"Please promise you will not fight today, but will see the chief."

The men agreed. To seal the promise they bowed down to the ground and poured dust on their heads while Risku still held the sandal.

Risku was happy with their promise, but the warriors were not satisfied. They clutched him by the arm and pointed toward the other village men.

"If *we* don't fight what will we do if they come to fight us?"

Risku agreed to return to the other side and talk with the villagers. He went back through the lines of swords and poisoned arrows to the men at the water hole. He explained to them that the Pulke men had agreed to talk to the chief instead of fighting. He talked with the men a long while and then taking the left sandal of their leader, he held it high in his hand. As they promised not to fight the Pulke men, the warriors stooped to the ground and poured dust over their heads to seal their promise, too.

Then Risku returned to his missionary friends, and the jeep with its peacemaker drove away.

We ought to obey God rather than men.

ACTS 5:29

A Man Who Could Not Yield

A new commander came to Fort Riley, Kansas. The news spread quickly through the stone barracks where the conscientious objectors were quartered. Instantly the same thought flashed through the minds of the men.

"What kind of a commander will he be?"

Maurice Hess thought of the days they had only bread and water to eat and of the times they were served sour potatoes. He thought of the long winter days at Camp Meade in unheated barracks. He thought, too, of one commander they had had who understood conscientious objectors. He understood that working for the army in the camps at home was just as wrong as shooting the enemy in France. He had not asked them to wear uniforms or cook for the soldiers or work in the office. Maurice was very grateful for his understanding.

An officer once told him, "Maurice, the man who is running a typewriter is in the war as much as the man who is running a machine gun."

Maurice and his other 149 friends who were living at Fort Riley during the First World War did not need to wonder long about the kind of treatment they would get from the new commander. Very shortly the order came:

"Today the men in the stone barracks will police the parade grounds."

The CO's did not know what the new commander would do if they did not obey. But they refused as they had each time before, and waited for the commander's answer.

"Search every man. Take everything from him and throw him in the guardhouse," ordered the commander.

Forty-one men were crowded into a dirty little cell that was only large enough for twenty-two. There were no windows to let in air or light and all that entered came from the corridor above. Every day the concrete floor was flooded with water and, at night, the men had to sleep on it—still damp. Within a week, many were sick with influenza. The days passed slowly in the crowded cell, and the prisoners received their greatest comfort from reading their Bibles.

For several weeks the men endured the miserable conditions of the guardhouse. Then one day a truck backed up to the building and took a load of them down the road to Camp Funston. Day after day the truck returned for more until it was Maurice's turn. He and his friends were going to be tried in court because they could not do what the Bible and their consciences told them was wrong.

The truck entered the west gate of the camp and stopped in front of the trial barracks. When Maurice was ushered into the courtroom he found that all the members of the jury and all the court attendants were military officers. False witnesses were ready to testify against him.

When his turn came, Maurice stood before the court. Turning to the officers, he spoke clearly and firmly:

"I am a young man and life looks good to me. I want to go out into the world and make use of what little talent I have.

"But I know that first of all I must obey God. I know the teaching of Christ, my Saviour. He taught us to love our enemies. . . . He didn't only teach this; Jesus showed that He loved His enemies when He died on the cross.

"We say that we are Christians. Only hypocrites would turn back because of taunts and jeers. I would rather go to prison or be tortured or put to death than take part in the war. We cannot yield or compromise; we must suffer."

The room was still when Maurice paused. He continued. "Two hundred years ago our people were persecuted in Germany. They came to America where our Constitution says all may worship and obey God as the Bible teaches.

"If the authorities think this should be changed, then all we can do is endure persecution.

"I do not refuse to suffer or die. I pray God for strength to remain faithful."

Maurice had made his defense and he could only wait for the court to decide. Anxious moments followed, but the testimonies of Maurice and his friends seemed of no use. The CO's were sentenced to twenty-five years at Fort Leavenworth Prison.

A heavy guard transported the sober group of fellows to the military prison. There was no laughter or merrymaking —only serious thoughts about what was awaiting them. Stories that had leaked out about Fort Leavenworth had always been dreadful.

On their arrival they were searched and after a few days of prison routine were assigned to prison work. Once again Maurice refused, because as his friend said,

"The work of the military prison is all military work and this institution is used to discipline disobedient soldiers. If I could accept the work in this prison I could have accepted the work of the army."

Immediately they were taken to solitary confinement where they received only bread and water for fourteen days. The following two weeks they received full meals, then the diet was again bread and water for fourteen days. That's the way it alternated. Maurice learned to pick out the crusts of bread and chew them well. He did not throw away a third-handed turkey leg, because by long sucking he could taste a little fat.

For nine hours a day he stood by the gate of his cell, handcuffed to the iron bars. At nighttime there was only the cold concrete floor for a bed. The days were long and tiring, and night brought little rest.

One day a colonel from Washington visited the "Hole" as it was called, and hearing the pleas of the boys, ordered their Bibles returned. Then during the long hours while he was chained to the bars Maurice read the familiar passages that brought him comfort and peace.

After the war was over and the armistice signed, 109 conscientious objectors were released from Fort Leaven-

worth. Among them was Maurice Hess. He left the prison
for his home January 27, 1919. Not long afterward, he was
asked to teach in a Brethren college and for years he has
helped the young·people of his church. He writes this to
youth today:

"It is my hope and prayer that all of you will learn how
many Christians suffered because they obeyed God. May the
lives of all those who have died for Christ give you strength
for the tests that will come to you."

Resist not evil . . . give to him that asketh thee.

MATTHEW 5:39, 42

The Wells of Trouble

Isaac was concerned about his flocks and herds that were grazing on the rolling plains. They could not live without water. For days no rain had fallen on the land of Canaan. The tender shoots of grass turned brown and the running streams became dry beds. The water in the wells sank lower every day.

Isaac remembered how, years before, his father Abraham had gone to Egypt during a famine to feed his flocks on the rich grasslands watered by the river Nile. He too would go to the land of wealth and plenty to save the flocks his father had given him.

But God was not pleased with Isaac's plan. He spoke to Isaac, saying, "Do not go down to Egypt; dwell in the land

7

of which I shall tell you. Sojourn in this land, and I will be with you, and will bless you. . . . "

Isaac obeyed God and pitched his tents in Gerar, in the land of the Philistines. Here his herdsmen found pastureland, and Isaac's flocks multiplied and his herds grew.

Here, too, Isaac found good soil to grow grain. While the herdsmen were watching the flocks, other servants were busy tending the fields. In those days men plowed with wooden plows and scattered the seeds from the skirts of their tunics. Sunshine and rain fed the planted fields, and servants guarded the sprouting grain from the flocks of birds and choking weeds. Then came the time of harvest. Isaac looked at the ripened grain and saw that God had blessed him with a hundredfold harvest. He became very rich.

Abimelech, the King of the Philistines, was also watching Isaac's fields. He saw the pasturelands dotted with sheep and goats. He saw the hundredfold harvest and the great store of servants.

"Surely this man has become powerful," he thought. And Abimelech envied Isaac.

Isaac's Philistine neighbors envied him too. They knew that Isaac could not live without water, so they filled up Isaac's wells which had been dug by his father, Abraham.

Abimelech saw what was happening. He understood the jealousy of his people. So he called Isaac and said, "Go away from us, for you are much mightier than we."

When Isaac heard the king's orders he called his great household together and they traveled eastward to the dry valley of Gerar. Here they pitched their tents by the stopped-up wells of his father Abraham. Quickly the servants re-opened the wells and once again there was water for the thirsty household. Isaac called the wells by the old names which Abraham had given them.

The servants also dug a new well in the valley and found springing water. But when Abimelech's herdsmen who were tending their flocks in the same valley saw them using the new well, they became very angry.

"The water is ours," they told Isaac's herdsmen. But the servants who had dug the well claimed it for Isaac.

When word of the trouble reached Isaac, he said, "I will call the name of this well Esek (E'sĕk) because Abimelech's herdsmen and my herdsmen quarreled for it."

Then he called his servants together and said, "We will leave this place of trouble and strife."

Immediately the household moved up the valley in search of new pastureland where they would be undisturbed by the Philistine herdsmen. Isaac's servants dug another well and again found pure water.

Abimelech's herdsmen, still not far away, saw the well of springing water and said among themselves, "The water is ours."

Again there was trouble between the herdsmen of Isaac and the herdsmen of Abimelech.

When word of the quarrel reached the ears of Isaac, he named the well Sitnah, because Abimelech's servants and his servants had trouble and contention over it.

Once more the tents were taken down and Isaac left the well of trouble for new pastures far up the valley. Here the servants re-opened the wells of father Abraham and dug yet another new well. Now the flocks and herds, Isaac's servants and his family all had water. And this time Abimelech's servants did not take the well.

When Isaac saw the Philistine herdsmen had given up, he said, "I will call this well Rehoboth (Rĕ-hō′both) for now the Lord hath made room for us and we shall be fruitful in the land."

During the same night the Lord appeared to Isaac and said, "I am the God of Abraham your father: fear not, for I am with you, and will bless you, and multiply your descendants for my servant Abraham's sake."

Isaac built an altar there and thanked God for taking care of him and his flocks.

When Abimelech saw that God was pleased with Isaac, he was afraid. He knew he had treated Isaac unfairly when he sent him away from Gerar. He feared that Isaac might try to get even now that he was so powerful, so Abimelech decided to pay him a visit. He called his friend Ahuzzeth (A-hŭz'ath) and his chief captain Phicol (Fī'col) and together they traveled to the place Isaac had pitched his tents.

Isaac wondered when he saw his guests coming. "Why do you come to me, seeing you hate me and have sent me away from you?" he asked.

And they answered, "We see plainly that the Lord is with you so we say let there be an oath between you and us, and let us make a covenant with you, that you will do us no harm just as we have not touched you and we have done nothing but good and have sent you away in peace. You are now the blessed of the Lord."

Immediately Isaac ordered his servants to prepare a feast for the Philistine King and his friends. When the banquet was ended they all retired for the night.

The following morning Isaac and Abimelech arose and made a covenant. They promised each other they would be friends. Then they parted in peace.

Later that day Isaac's servants came to him saying, "We again found water when we were digging a well."

Then Isaac knew that once more God was pleased with him. He thanked God for the well and named it Sheba. The name of the city is called Beersheba even today.

And ye shall be hated of all men for my name's sake: but he that endureth to the end the same shall be saved.

MATTHEW 10:22

He Followed His Footsteps

This is the story of a brave man—a man named Joris Wippe—a man who dared to be an Anabaptist. In those long ago days when Joris lived, everyone belonged to the same church. Whenever a baby was born he was baptized and from that time on he was a member of the church. Being a member of the church did not make one a Christian.

The church continued this way for many years, partly because most people could not learn the truth from Bibles because they were written in Latin. Only the priests could read Latin. And unfortunately even the priests seldom bothered to read their Bibles.

One day Menno Simons, a priest from Holland, began to study his Bible. During the months he had been training to become a priest, he had never read it. Now he found out,

95

from his New Testament, that being baptized as a baby and going to mass every Sunday does not make you a Christian. He read in his Bible that a sinner is a person who disobeys God and does things his own way.

"That is what I am," thought Menno Simons. "I am a sinner. I don't care about pleasing God and doing His work, but I spend my time and my money to please myself."

Menno had been doing just what other priests did. He offered the mass, listened to the confessions of the people and prayed for the living and the dead. Then he spent his free hours drinking and playing cards.

He read more in his Bible. He found that God will forgive anyone who has disobeyed Him if he is really sorry for the way he has acted and tells God so. God can do that because He gave Jesus to die for all the sins of all the people in the world. Menno believed what he read in his Bible. He believed that Jesus died to save him from being punished for his sin. He asked God to forgive him. From that time on Menno Simons obeyed God because he wanted to.

When Menno Simons realized what it really meant to be a Christian, he decided to leave the church and be baptized again. He felt that his baptism as a child was meaningless. And he wanted everybody to know that now his sinful life was washed clean.

There were others who believed as Menno did, so they met together to study God's Word. Their meetings were held in secret because their enemies determined that these Anabaptists (they called them Anabaptists because they were baptized again) should be punished for leaving the church. Some were burned to death; some were drowned; others were even put into lions' dens.

It was nearly twenty-two years after Menno Simons was rebaptized that this brave man, Joris Wippe (Joris Wip′pē), was put in prison for being an Anabaptist.

Joris sat in the dark, filthy prison of Dordrecht (Dort′-rĕcht), Holland. He knew that he was carefully guarded so he worked quickly. He must finish the letter before the guards found out what he was doing. They had taken away his ink to make letter writing impossible, but Joris found that mulberry juice was a good substitute. He knew he would die soon and he was writing his last message to his sons.

> My most beloved sons, all three of you, you are well aware now, I trust, that I am in bonds here for the testimony of Christ our Saviour, . . . and wait with patience daily, . . . to offer up my body and soul to the magnifying of His holy name. . . . Now it is the will of the Lord that we must part; but let it not grieve you. For if you . . . keep His commandments all the days of your life, we shall hereafter meet in one fold. . . . Comfort your mother, and often, when you have time, read to her a chapter or two. And spend the time which God gives you, in all sobriety and righteousness, with prayer and supplication to God, that He would keep you from the evil. . . . Be not terrified; for the Lord your God is with you wherever you go, and will be your Protector. . . .

Joris was not able to write many letters to his family, because he was so carefully guarded, but he thought of them often and spent many of the long days praying for them. He also spent long hours thinking of the happy times he should soon have with his Lord in heaven. He loved his family, but for one who had suffered as he had, life with Christ seemed dearer.

Day after day he waited to hear what his sentence would be, but the lords who had arrested him were strangely silent. These lords were in trouble. Even before they arrested Joris they knew he was a good man. They had not wanted to harm him, but they put him in jail because the monks and priests persuaded them to.

Before the lords sent Joris the summons to go to jail, they thought to themselves, "Joris will leave the country when he hears that he is to go to prison. Then the monks and priests will let us alone and Joris will be safe too."

But they were shocked and dismayed when Joris appeared when they sent him the summons. There was nothing they could do but put him in prison. Now they must decide what to do with him.

While Joris waited in prison and his family waited anxiously at home, the lords tried to find some excuse for setting this good man free.

"Let us send him to the court at The Hague (Hāg) in Holland to be tried," they said. "Perhaps they will set him free."

But the lords at The Hague returned him to Dordrecht, saying, "Joris Wippe must be tried in Dordrecht because that is his home town."

The lords of Dordrecht could do nothing now. Finally, after months of waiting the death sentence was pronounced.

> Sentence of death of Joris Wippe done and pronounced in the chamber [of Justice], the 4th of August, 1558.

> Whereas Joris Wippe, Joosten's son, born at Meenen, in Flanders, has dared to have himself rebaptized, and has held pernicious views concerning baptism, according to testimony and truth, and all the evidence which the Judges and the council have seen and heard with regard to it, and according to his own confession, therefore, he shall, to the honor of God, and the edification of the lords and the city, be drowned in a cask, and his body then be brought to the place of execution, and there be hung to the gallows, and his property shall be confiscated, and placed in the lord's exchequer.

The executioner was dismayed when he heard that it was his task to drown Joris. With tears in his eyes, he said, "How can I put to death this good man who has never harmed any one? He fed my wife and children many times. I cannot do it!"

Now the lords had more trouble, for no one wanted to carry out the sentence. For seven more weeks they searched for someone to take the executioner's place. Finally the thief catcher agreed to carry out the executioner's job. He filled a wine cask with water. Late on the night of October 1, 1558, he pushed Joris into the water where he drowned. The next day they hung his body by the feet where all the people could see it and mock. Thus at the age of 41, Joris gave his life for his Lord.

But Mrs. Wippe knew that her husband was glad to suffer and to die because shortly before his death he wrote to her:

> He [Christ] went before us with much misery and tribulation; we must follow His footsteps. . . . For He has so kindly admonished us . . . saying: If they have persecuted me, they will also persecute you. . . .

My little children, let us not love in word, neither in tongue; but in deed and in truth.

I John 3:18

Marie's Flight

Marie Fast stood in the doorway of her tent and looked down the long rows of tents stretching across the burning white sands of the Sinai Desert. Only nine months ago she had said good-by to her family in Minnesota and had come to the refugee camp at El Shatt to serve in relief work. Explosive mines in the Mediterranean had made the trip very dangerous.

During those first weeks in camp an epidemic of measles had broken out and an emergency ward was set up for nearly two hundred children. The workers became discouraged as they tried to care for sick children without enough bedding or clothing and little medicine. Nurses were few, too. The Yugoslav mothers and girls were hard-working and happy to help, but still there were problems, for the Yugoslav women and the nurses could not understand each other's language.

Marie's brother wrote that her church at home was praying for her and the other workers. Knowing that her many friends were remembering to pray gave her strong faith and courage when she felt weak and incapable.

The Mennonite Central Committee sent Marie to El Shatt to help these Yugoslavs who had been driven out of their homeland in 1943, during World War II. Hundreds of these families were living in small tent homes and getting food in tin buckets at a common cook tent. Thirty thousand refugees lived in the camp. They were hoping for the day when the fighting would stop and they could go home to beautiful Yugoslavia.

Marie was one of the seven relief workers who was chosen from the camp staff to accompany a shipload of refugees back to Yugoslavia. Going on these flights, as they were called, was a rare privilege and Marie was happy when she learned of her assignment.

Refugee women busily prepared for the journey home. They packed their few possessions into bags which they had made from scraps and canvas. Marie, too, packed the bag she would take with her, then sorted her remaining possessions, and, in her usual thorough manner packed them in her neatly arranged trunk.

Marie was eager for the trip. But she also knew it would be a serious responsibility. With all her eagerness she had a feeling she could not explain. Maybe she would never return. She sat down at the table, picked up her pen and began to write. When she had finished, Marie sealed the envelope and on the outside wrote carefully, "Just in case." Turning to her tentmate she said, "Helen, I wish you would keep this for me just in case I should never return from the flight."

Outside refugees were beginning to gather along the sandy track where the trucks would pick them up. A strange collection of bags and bundles lay in heaps beside their picturesque owners who were waiting for the signal to climb the steps to the seats on the back of the trucks.

Along the sandy track and in and out of the tents came sounds of joy. At last these people were leaving the bleak desert behind and going home. There was a feeling of sadness, too—the sadness that comes when friends who have endured much together must part, perhaps forever.

The good-byes were called and they started on their way: first by truck, then by box car, and finally across the Mediterranean in a troopship.

The five days on board ship were busy ones for the staff that traveled with the 1700 refugees. The doctor and two nurses prepared formulas for the babies, gave medicine to the patients in the ship's hospital, and did the endless tasks that make life easier for others.

The busy days passed one by one and the nights followed with welcome rest. The morning came when the ship neared port. Eager homecomers lined the decks searching out signs of land. A shout went up when they sighted the long gray shoreline, and excitement increased while it slowly changed into shops and houses and trees. The crowd of wanderers once again had come home.

Marie watched the refugees climb into the tiny boats that came to meet the ship. She saw one stagger under a clumsy bundle. Another held a wide-eyed youngster seeing his home for the first time. As Marie watched them leaving,

8

she thought of their bitter life on the desert and the care she had given them in sickness. Now she saw them come home, and she felt a new joy in her heart. She knew her life had been richer because she had lived with them.

The return voyage was restful for the seven relief workers. They were the only passengers until their ship would pick up German war prisoners in Italy. Then they would sail back to Port Said and take the overland trip to El Shatt.

The last night before the stop in Italy the troopship was pushing through rough waters that sent high waves breaking and spilling over her sides. Suddenly the ship gave a terrible lurch and the passengers sat up in bed. The boat quivered as if some great monster had struck her. The emergency bell sounded and everyone raced to his life station.

"The ship has struck a mine," Marie heard as she reached her station. With trembling fingers she pulled on her life jacket. She struggled with the fasteners in the blackness. The feeble ray of an officer's flashlight scarcely penetrated the fog that surrounded him. The captain ordered, "Lower the lifeboats."

The huge waves pulled hard on the lifeboats as the men struggled with the cables which held them to the ship. The little boats rose on the crest of incoming waves and dropped back, pulling and straining on the cables which fastened them above.

Marie started down the rope ladder on the side of the ship. She clung tightly to the rungs as she groped her way in the darkness. Through the thick mist she could scarcely see her way. The lifeboat swayed and rolled on the huge waves. Just as she reached to climb in, the boat whisked away. Then back it came, rushing in upon her. Again and again Marie

tried to get into the lifeboat, but always the great waves drove it from her reach.

Finally she struggled back up the ladder to the deck. The crewmen lowered a second boat even with the deck. A lieutenant and Marie climbed in and were slowly lowered toward the rough sea. The boat rose high on the crest of a wave, then crashing downward, snapped one of the cables and spilled Marie and the lieutenant into the black waters. Those still on deck watched helplessly as the waves swirled them away.

They appeared once on the crest of a wave, and the lieutenant was holding Marie. Above the roar of the waves he called to the figures on deck, "We're all right." Then they sank away in the darkness.

Days later the lieutenant's body was found washed ashore, but Marie was never seen again.

Marie's assignment was done. She had cared for the wandering suffering ones and had seen them home. Though she had lost her own life by one of war's weapons, Marie had helped to heal a few of its wounds.

And we ought to lay down our lives for the brethren.

I JOHN 3:16

He Went to Russia

Clayton Kratz could have written a good long paper on the Mennonites of Russia for the church history teacher in college. He knew how Catherine the Great, a cruel woman but a clever ruler, had invited them to come over from Germany and farm the open countryland. They had come on her promise of free transportation, free lands, and religious liberty. He had read the story of the early hardships of those 228 first families on the new frontier back in the 1870's. He knew how God had blessed their thrift and hard work until by 1914, one hundred thousand of them lived in comfortable homesteads. He had seen pictures of their prosperous farms and their wheat fields waving across a million acres of Russian plains.

Somehow he'd been thinking about these Russian Mennonites a lot since they had sung, "Faith of Our Fathers" at Blooming Glen Church that summer Sunday morning. That song was meaning more to Russian Mennonite boys than to him, Clayton thought. For tragedy had swept Russia. The rich people were suffering and the poor were going hungry. The trouble had hit the rolling wheat fields of the Mennonite settlers. Although World War I was over, the soldiers of Russia didn't return home to live in peace, for inside all of Russia a war had broken out—a civil war. The people were tired of war. Clayton had heard of the terrible ruin— buildings destroyed, strong men killed, fine farming land trampled down as the armies battled back and forth. And to add to the misery, the rains hadn't come. What few crops the soldiers hadn't trampled down were scorched by the sun. Russia had never seen a worse famine.

The people of Russia, thin and hungry, clothed in rags, were calling, *"Chleb! Chleb!"* "Bread, in God's name, bread!" Their cry sounded through all Russia. A message came to America:

American Mennonites must send help to our Russian brothers.

Clayton Kratz had learned to begin each day with "morning watch," a period of prayer and Bible reading. In school he studied well. He was a leader among his college friends. He had one more year of college and after graduation he wanted to be a teacher. This last year he was going to lead the Christian service activities of the students. Clayton looked forward to the best year yet.

While he was getting ready for the big year a letter came from the Mennonite Central Committee which said to Clayton, "Will you go to Russia in relief work?" In spite of all that the big year held for him, Clayton answered, "Yes, I'll go to Russia." He had sung, "Faith of our fathers, we will love both friend and foe." Being faithful to that promise meant going to Russia for Clayton. Instead of heading for college in September, 1920, Clayton boarded the ship, *Providence,* and set sail for Russia. And he went singing, "Faith of our fathers, holy faith, I will be true to thee till death."

Traveling in wartime Russia was difficult and dangerous. The first trip by train lay right near the battleground of the Red and White Armies. In the evening Clayton and his friend Orie Miller took a third class coach which had the windows boarded shut against the cold. "There's a hard winter ahead," they told each other.

By the dim light of some flickering candles the men stowed their baggage on the narrow shelf near the ceiling of the car. They made crude beds on the wooden benches before the last candle sputtered and died. It was dark. The train rumbled on into the night, carrying them deeper and deeper into the heart of suffering Russia.

While the two young relief workers slept in their darkened coach new passengers found their way into the train. At each station stop crowds of poorly dressed refugees waited to return to the towns and villages which General Wrangel and his White Army had just recently captured from the Red Army. In a mass they pushed slowly toward the train. They were too starved to hurry, but a few always managed to slip past the conductor into the already crowded coaches. By morning the aisles were jammed with passengers sitting and standing, surrounded by bundles of baggage. Some rode on top of the train. Some even hung on the sides, getting the full force of the bitter wind.

Clayton looked at the pitifully dressed peasants with only cloth or string shoes. Then he looked out of the window of the moving train. The deserted villages with their empty houses told the grim story of the famine. It had touched everyone. When the food and grain were gone, the farmers had fed the straw-thatched roofs of their houses and barns to the horse and cow, and finally left in search of food for themselves. The roadways were lined with the peasant farmers fighting to live. Their cries echoed and re-echoed across Russia, *"Chleb! Chleb!"*

Clayton and Orie thought of the warm suits and shoes and stockings which waited to be unpacked. They thought of the money which would buy milk for the babies and food for their parents. How they ached to reach the colonies and begin their work.

By nightfall they arrived at Halbstadt, the first Mennonite colony. They listened to the sad stories of families who had lost their homes and businesses because of the fighting armies. Then as they met with the leaders of the colony, Orie said, "Make a list of the things which you need right now and which $10,000 will buy." When the men of the colony had listed their needs their leader said, "But the Chortitza colonies have been in the path of both armies and have suffered terribly. We want you to help them first and then we will take what is left."

"Such unselfish people," said Clayton. "They need food and clothing so badly, but they think of others first."

The following day Brother Peters, their host, was unable to find a team to make the seventy-mile trip to the next village because no one was anxious to give up his horse for fear the soldiers would seize it out on the open road. Brother Peters had been a wealthy man and the owner of 2,000 acres of land, but he had lost it in the war. Now only two of his forty-four horses remained so he also hesitated driving the team through. But on finding no others, he offered them, and the three men began the trip to Alexandrowsk early in the afternoon.

The road from Halbstadt to Alexandrowsk ran straight with the battle line where General Wrangel was desperately holding back the Red Army. This road itself had seen fighting only four weeks before. By the side of it lay hundreds of horses, some partly eaten by the dogs and some as they had fallen. Hundreds of mounds of earth silently told a sadder story of the soldiers who had fallen in battle.

By nightfall they reached Alexandrowsk at the side of the Dnieper River. From these people they listened to the sad stories of missing sons and ruined homes. They again made plans to help their suffering friends.

Early the next morning Clayton and Orie were awakened by the rumbling sound of wagons and hundreds of marching feet on the street outside their window. The stream of loaded wagons continued for hours, carrying burdens of horse feed, cooking apparatus, huge guns, and ammunition away from the territory just lately captured by the Reds.

"These are the retreating White troops coming from the other side of the Dnieper River," thought the men as they watched from their bedroom window. They could hear the band playing in the distance and the sound of soldiers singing Russian war songs as they marched past the building. Always in the background was the low rumble of cannon-fire, but the Americans were not alarmed for they supposed it to belong to the retreating Whites.

After their breakfast of coffee and bread and honey, Clayton and Orie made plans for the day. Orie had just begun writing in his diary when Brother Peters returned with news from the army. "The shots which we hear from across the River belong to the Reds. We must leave the colony at once because the Reds are advancing rapidly on us."

The men quickly collected their belongings. Orie boarded a hospital train leaving for the South, while Clayton and Brother Peters returned to Halbstadt by carriage.

Once more at Halbstadt, Clayton worked with Brother

Peters helping to plan for distributing the food and clothing. As long as the White Army held back the Reds he could work in safety. But before long news came from the North that the Whites were weakening. Brother Peters knew that meant Halbstadt would soon be taken. "The village will fall," he said to Clayton. "If you are here when the Reds take over you will be taken prisoner."

Did this mean Clayton must leave the work he had just begun? "I have done no harm," he thought. "No one would have cause to harm me." Yet he knew it would be reckless to stay in the threatened village, so he made plans to leave. Brother Peters harnessed fine running horses, ready for flight the following morning. Everything was prepared. He would escape at the crack of dawn. But while the household slept the Reds entered the village. The villagers awoke at dawn to find themselves in the hands of the Red Army. Clayton's hope for escape was gone. He was taken as a spy.

The people of the village pleaded for him and he was released and able to work. But his freedom lasted only twelve days. One day a messenger rushed to Brother Peters with the news that Clayton had again been arrested. Word of the arrest spread quickly through the colony, but no one knew where he had been taken. Finally, word came from a man in a near-by colony. "They were taking him through Wernersdorf when I spoke with him," said the man. "He was not afraid and seemed ready to go wherever the officers took him."

Brother Peters continued the search for many weeks, but nowhere could he find a trace of his missing friend. American Mennonite workers later joined the search, but the young relief worker was never found. Some think he was shot by the Red Army. He may have become sick and died. He may have been sent to a Siberian mine.

No one will ever know where Clayton Kratz now lies buried. But in the cemetery of the Blooming Glen Mennonite Church in Bucks County, Pennsylvania, stands a stone with the simple inscription:

Memorial
Clayton H. Kratz
Born November 5, 1896
Went to Russia, 1920

Live peaceably with all men.

ROMANS 12:18

The Christ of the Andes

Once again, men talked of war in Argentina. This was nothing new—the people of Argentina were used to disputes over land—disputes that usually led to that ugly climax, war. This time the quarrel was about the boundary line between Argentina and Chile, high in the Andes Mountains. Chile thought it should be at the place where the mountains divide the water, making some of it flow east and some flow west. Argentina wanted more land. She thought it should go from one high peak to the next. Year after year the countries quarreled about the boundary line, and year after year they became more and more angry. Finally in 1898 they began to build battleships and raise large armies.

President Roca did not want his country to fight Chile. He thought of the great cattle ranches and the vast wheat fields. He thought of the huge stretches of corn and oats and alfalfa and the vineyards near the foothills of the mountains. They were among the finest in the world. They were making his country rich. President Roca also knew that if Argentina spent all its money for an army, she would soon become very poor.

"We must do something to stop this trouble before it is too late," he thought.

Someone else did not want Argentina to go to war. Bishop Benavente (Bĕn-a-vĕn′tē) knew it would make his country poor, and he also knew it was wrong to kill others. Earnestly he told the people of Buenos Aires that war was wicked.

"Let us be friendly to our neighbors," he said. "We don't want war."

This surprised the people of Buenos Aires. Some of them did not agree with Bishop Benavente, but others thought to themselves, "He is right. Could we not settle this without war?"

The bishop traveled up and down the country day after day, telling people, "We do not need war to settle our quarrel. Let us do it peacefully and be friends."

News of what Bishop Benavente was saying leaked across the border to Chile. Soon a Chilean bishop started up and down *his* country asking *his* people, "Couldn't we settle this quarrel without war? War is sin."

Before long many people in both countries realized that it is wrong to hate others. The women begged their husbands not to join the army. Finally so many people wanted peace that they sent messages to their presidents saying, "Let us decide our quarrel peacefully. We don't want war."

Great Britain was interested in Argentina because many of her own people were living there. When she heard of the trouble she offered to help Argentina and Chile decide where the boundary line should be. Both countries were pleased to have Great Britain help them and agreed to accept her decision.

As soon as King Edward VII decided this question, Chile sold the warships she had been building and paid all her debts. She even had some money left to improve her country. A few years later she built a railroad across the mountains to Argentina.

Argentina and Chile were glad that they did not need to go to war to settle their quarrel. "We ought to remember this happy solution in some special way," they said.

So both countries brought their old bronze cannons to the arsenal at Buenos Aires. There the metal was melted and a great artist worked day after day, shaping it into a beautiful statue of Christ. The people wanted a statue of Him to remind them of their peace with each other because Jesus is the true peacemaker.

The people waited eagerly for the day the statue would be finished. As they waited, they thought about a place for it to stand. Why not put it on the very highest mountain in the Andes where it could be seen from both countries? There it would remind everyone that peace is stronger than war. Years before, a little stone house had been built in which travelers could find protection from the cold as they crossed the mountains. Surely, this would be a wonderful place for the beautiful statue of the Man who loved peace.

Finally, in March, 1904, the Christ of the Andes was finished and ready to go to its new home on the highest peak

in the Andes Mountains. It traveled 654 miles by train, then mules pulled it on up the steep mountain road. When the wild mountainside became too rugged even for mules, hundreds of soldiers and sailors from both Argentina and Chile pulled it the rest of the way with ropes.

In the meantime thousands of people were making preparations to go to the Andes to see the statue and celebrate together. Some traveled many weeks to get there. Others camped beside the mountain for days waiting for the dedication day to come.

At last, on March 13, the excited crowd gathered. First of all the people from Argentina stepped across the boundary line into Chile. And the people from Chile stepped across into Argentina. Then everyone looked toward the statue that stood between them. There, standing huge and tall on a round pedestal representing the world, was the beautiful figure of Christ. In His left hand He held a cross. His right hand was stretched out as if He were blessing the three thousand people who had come to celebrate. At the bottom of the statue were these words:

"Sooner shall these mountains crumble to dust than Argentines and Chileans break the peace which at the feet of Christ the Redeemer they have sworn to maintain."

Cannons roared and bands played. The sound echoed and re-echoed through the mountains. When the last note died away in the distance, Bishop Anoud (Än′ōōd) said:

"We dedicate this monument to Argentina and Chile and to the whole world. May we learn its lesson of peace."

Then as the people bowed their heads, the Archbishop of Argentina prayed:

" . . . Protect, Lord, our country. Ever give unto us faith and hope. Let our first inheritance be the peace which shall bear fruit, and let its fine example be its greatest glory, so that the souls of those who have known Thee shall be able to bring forth from Thee all forms of blessing for the two Americas. Amen."

Acknowledgments

The stories which are found in this book were based on material gathered from books, magazine articles, information received from informed individuals, and in some instances were adapted from accounts already written in story form. As far as the writer was able to learn, the chief incidents in each story are true. The conversation, however, is fictional although it attempts to carry faithfully the spirit of the characters. Descriptive materials added to the story were obtained through research into the customs and local color of the times. The sources are listed below.

Without the help of many kind people who shared their experiences and gave their time in critical reading of the stories, and without the permission of the following publishers to use their materials, this book would have been impossible. Each one deserves our deepest thanks.

A Man Who Could Not Yield

Rufus D. Bowman, *The Church of the Brethren and War.* Elgin, Illinois. Brethren Publishing House, 1944.

An Ill Wind

The Children's Story Caravan. Collected by a Committee of the Philadelphia Yearly Meeting of Friends, Anna Pettit Broomell, chairman; Philadelphia and London: J. B. Lippincott Co., 1935.

At the Wrong End of the Rifle

D. M. Gill and A. M. Pullen, *Victories of Peace.* New York: Friendship Press, 1936.

He Followed His Footsteps

Thieleman J. van Braght, *Martyrs' Mirror.* The Mennonite Publishing Co., Elkhart, Indiana, 1886.

He Went to Russia

Information received from the diary of Orie O. Miller, Akron, Pa.

Jacob Decides

Harvey Hostetler, *Descendants of Barbara Hostetler,* Scottdale, Pa., Mennonite Publishing House, 1938.

On Corridor Two

E. J. Swalm, *Nonresistance Under Test.* Cober Printing Service, Kitchener, Ontario, 1935.

Pastor John

An unpublished article by Rufus Franz, *Resist Not Evil, An Experience of a Mennonite Minister in Time of War,* filed in the Mennonite Central Committee Archives, Akron, Pa.

Peter's Plea

From the article, "My Recollections of P. M. Friesen," *Mennonite Life,* October, 1948.

The Mystery of the Thatch

John Horsch, *The Principle of Nonresistance as Held by the Mennonite Church.* Mennonite Publishing House, Scottdale, Pa., 1939.

The Christ of the Andes

Erica Dunkerley and Roderic Dunkerley, *The Arm of God,* Oliphants Ltd., 21 Paternoster Square, London, E.C. (Book is out of print.)

Marie's Flight

Samuel Yoder, *Middle-East Sojourn.* The Herald Press, Scottdale, Pa., 1952. Letters to Elizabeth Bauman from Mrs. Delvin Kirchhofer, Mrs. Leland Harder, Grace Augsburger. Interviews with Samuel Yoder and Dr. C. Richard Yoder.

The Man in the Saffron Robe

D. M. Gill and A. M. Pullen, *Victories of Peace.* New York: Friendship Press, 1936.

The Peacemaker

Leland S. Brubaker, "With Our Visitors in Africa," *Gospel Messenger,* Elgin, Illinois, June 7, 1947, 96:20-21.

The film, *Risku Tells You His Story,* General Mission Board, Church of the Brethren, Elgin, Illinois.

The Pick and Shovel Army
    D. M. Gill and A. M. Pullen, *Victories of Peace*. New York: Friendship Press, 1936.

The Price of Loyalty
    G. F. Hershberger, *War, Peace, and Nonresistance*. Scottdale, Pa., The Herald Press, 1944.

The Wells of Trouble
    The Holy Bible, Genesis 26:1-33.

The Author

The Peace Problems Committee of the Mennonite Church might easily have expected that Elizabeth Hershberger Bauman would know all the facts and stories about Mennonites' belief in love and nonresistance when they asked her to write *Coals of Fire*. For Elizabeth's father has known and written many papers and books on these subjects. His *War, Peace, and Nonresistance* is especially well known.

Mrs. Bauman was born in Kalona, Iowa, July 11, 1924. She grew up in Goshen, Indiana. Here she went to grade school and high school. She attended Goshen College and received her B.S. in Education and B.A. in Bible degrees in 1946. Then she taught school for two years. Mrs. Bauman lives in Goshen, Indiana, and is a pastor's wife and the mother of two sons.